CAFE

ASSESSMENT *to* INSTRUCTION

Get Ready, Assess, and Teach Every Student
A Successful Way Forward to Literacy

Educational Design, LLC
1911 SW Campus Drive #683
Federal Way, WA 98023
www.thedailycafe.com

Library of Congress Cataloging in Publication Data Pending

ISBN 978-1-61892-009-6

Cover and interior design by Madeline Boushey

Manufactured in the United States of America

View handouts:
www.thedailycafe.com/articles/2017-CAFE-Workshop-Handouts

Welcome

Teaching students is both exciting and challenging.

Witnessing the flashes of brilliance that make way for grasping and mastering skills is truly rewarding. The challenges we face as teachers are not new. We know there are no overnight fixes, no magic wands, and no one-size-fits-all programs that can ensure the growth of each of our students. Like you, we allow these challenges to motivate us to become the best teachers we can be.

Exceptional teachers have tenacity—resilience to overcome adversity, passion to stay the course, and perseverance to find strategies that will help each student succeed. Every day when we are working with children, and even when our classrooms are empty, we dig deeper to find these strategies. And when we realize that we need more help, we care enough to learn new skills, replenish our stamina, and teach again. Thank you for joining us today to learn, refresh, and replenish your skills with CAFE.

Let's get started!

Contents

STARTING OUT

CAFE OVERVIEW

CAFE MENU

ACCOUNTABILITY

CAFE SYSTEM

CAFE RESOURCES

RESOURCES

REFLECTION

STARTING OUT

CAFE OVERVIEW

CAFE MENU

ACCOUNTABILITY

CAFE SYSTEM

CAFE RESOURCES

RESOURCES

REFLECTION

Daily 5 and CAFE Self-Assessment

Indicate your knowledge of the following using a 1, 2, 3, or 4.
1=New to Me 2=Have Questions 3=Got It 4=Applying

DAILY 5 + MATH DAILY 3

Daily 5

- ☐ Set up Read to Self, including support lessons
- ☐ Set up Work on Writing, including support lessons
- ☐ Set up Read to Someone, including support lessons
- ☐ Set up Word Work, including support lessons
- ☐ Set up Listen to Reading, including support lessons
- ☐ Barometer Child
- ☐ Planning foundation lessons

Student Choice

- ☐ Building stamina
- ☐ Handing off Daily 5 choice to students
- ☐ Supporting student book choice
- ☐ Supporting student writing choice

Sharing and Celebrating

- ☐ Setting up the structure

Classroom Design

- ☐ Whole-group and small-group meeting area
- ☐ Classroom library
- ☐ Student work space
- ☐ Teacher area
- ☐ Setting up the CAFE Menu

CAFE

Focus Lessons

- ☐ Skill and strategy instruction
- ☐ Short and explicit
- ☐ Student engagement during instruction

Small Group

- ☐ Grouping students by skills and strategies
- ☐ Keeping the lesson short—what is the structure?
- ☐ Record keeping and grading
- ☐ Resources in our school and beyond

Conferring

- ☐ Setting up conferring notebook
- ☐ Touch Points and grading
- ☐ Using the CAFE Menu to support decisions or strategy

Assessing

- ☐ Administering reading assessments
- ☐ Analyzing assessment data and setting student goals
- ☐ Setting up assessment materials and student assessment

Whole Group

- ☐ Developing Curriculum Calendar
- ☐ Using CAFE and Curriculum Calendar to design lessons
- ☐ Understanding interactive read-aloud, teaching skills, and strategies

NEW TO ME — HAVE QUESTIONS — GOT IT — APPLYING

STARTING OUT

CAFE OVERVIEW

CAFE MENU

ACCOUNTABILITY

CAFE SYSTEM

CAFE RESOURCES

RESOURCES

REFLECTION

CAFE Literacy System Overview

System for engaging students in their reading achievement

SYSTEM FOR...

- **analyzing student learning,**
- **determining goals and strategies,**
- **recording instructional plans, and**
- **instructing whole groups, small groups, and individuals**

Reflection . . .

Literacy Components: Then and Now

	THEN (40+ years ago)			DAILY 5	NOW
PURPOSE	We will all get through the story.	Kids must feel good about themselves. We will all get through the story with help.	Every child deserves to be taught on their level during the day.		Students learn reading strategies to access text.
STRUCTURE	Seat Work	Centers	Workshop		Daily 5
RESOURCE	Basal One anthology	Basal One anthology Class sets of trade books	Basal anthology Trade books children could read		Basal anthology Book rooms Library books of choice
CLASSROOM LIBRARY	None	100 books	Larger, leveled		Goal of over 1,000 books in each class library, organized by genre
GROUPING	Whole-group Leveled reading groups	Whole-group heterogeneous reading groups	Whole-group guided reading Walk to read		Whole group, small group, one-on-one
ACCESS TO TEXT	Round robin. Student might not be able to read the text.	Round robin. Student might not be able to read the text.	Each student reads text he or she can read.		Teach skills and strategies so student can read any text. Each student has text he or she can read independently.

Reflection . . .

NEW TO ME — HAVE QUESTIONS — GOT IT — APPLYING

STARTING OUT

CAFE OVERVIEW

CAFE MENU

ACCOUNTABILITY

CAFE SYSTEM

CAFE RESOURCES

RESOURCES

REFLECTION

The CAFE Menu

COMPREHENSION I understand what I read	ACCURACY I can read the words	FLUENCY I can read accurately, with expression, and understand what I read	EXPAND VOCABULARY I know, find, and use interesting words
STRATEGIES	**STRATEGIES**	**STRATEGIES**	**STRATEGIES**
Check for understanding	Abundant easy reading	Voracious reading	Voracious reading
Back up and reread	Look carefully at letters and words	Read appropriate-level texts that are a good fit	Tune in to interesting words and use new vocabulary in speaking and writing
Use prior knowledge to connect with text	Cross checking . . . Do the pictures and/or words look right? Do they sound right? Do they make sense?	Reread text	Use prior knowledge and context to predict and confirm meaning
Make and adjust predictions; use text to confirm	Flip the sound	Practice common sight words and high-frequency words	Use pictures, illustrations, and diagrams
Infer and support with evidence	Use the pictures . . . Do the words and pictures match?	Adjust and apply different reading rates to match text	Use word parts to determine the meaning of words (prefixes, suffixes, origins, abbreviations, etc.)
Make a picture or mental image	Use beginning and ending sounds	Use punctuation to enhance phrasing and prosody (end marks, commas, etc.)	Ask someone to define the word for you
Monitor and fix up	Blend sounds; stretch and reread	Read text as the author would say it, conveying the meaning or feeling	Use dictionaries, thesauruses, and glossaries as tools
Ask questions throughout the reading process	Chunk letters and sounds together		
Use text features (titles, headings, captions, graphic features)	Skip the word, then come back		
Summarize text; include sequence of main events	Trade a word/guess a word that makes sense		
Use main idea and supporting details to determine importance	Recognize words at sight		
Determine and analyze author's purpose and support with text			
Recognize literary elements (genre, plot, character, setting, problem/resolution, theme)			
Recognize and explain cause-and-effect relationships			
Compare and contrast within and between text			

BEHAVIORS THAT SUPPORT READING

Get started right away · Stay in one spot · Work quietly · Read the whole time · Increase stamina · Ignore distractions · Persevere

The CAFE Menu for Emergent Readers

COMPREHENSION I listen to and understand stories that are read to me	ACCURACY I hear, work, and play with spoken language	FLUENCY I know letters, sounds, and words	EXPAND VOCABULARY I am aware of print and how to handle a book
STRATEGIES	**STRATEGIES**	**STRATEGIES**	**STRATEGIES**
Listen with understanding	Recognize when two words rhyme	Recognize uppercase letters	Identify front and back of book
Retell familiar stories using the pictures	Produce rhyming words	Recognize lowercase letters	Know where to begin reading
Tell a connected story using pictures	Orally blend words presented in syllable segments	Recognize sight words	Know to start reading at the top of a page
Retell story, including • story line—characters; • setting, problem, or goal events, sequencing beginning, middle, end	Clap words in a sentence		Know sentences and words are read left to right
Respond to questions about the story	Clap syllables in one to three segments		When finished with left page, move on to right page
	Blend onset and rime		Know return sweep when reading a sentence
	Orally match words that begin with the same sound		Word-by-word matching
	Orally match words that end with the same sound		Understand concept of a word
	Identify the first sound in a word		Understand concept of a letter
	Identify the last sound in a word		Know there are spaces between words
	Blend two sounds to make a word		Know the meaning of a period
	Blend three sounds to make a word		
	Segment three sounds in a word		

BEHAVIORS THAT SUPPORT READING

Get started right away　Stay in one spot　Work quietly　Read the whole time　Increase stamina

The CAFE Menu Aligned to Common Core

To view grades K–8, visit the CAFE Menu section of TheDailyCAFE.com.

LINKED TO SECOND-GRADE COMMON CORE STANDARDS*

COMPREHENSION	ACCURACY	FLUENCY	EXPAND VOCABULARY
STRATEGIES	**STRATEGIES**	**STRATEGIES**	**STRATEGIES**
Use prior knowledge to connect with text RL.2.1	Abundant easy reading RL.2.10, RI.2.10	Voracious reading RF.2.10, RI.2.10	Voracious reading RL.2.10, RI.2.10
Make and adjust predictions; use text to confirm RL.2.1	Look carefully at letters and words RF.2.3	Read appropriate-level texts that are a good fit RL.2.10, RI.2.4, RI.2.10, RF.2.4	Tune in to interesting words and use new vocabulary in speaking and writing L.2.4
Infer and support with evidence RI.2.1, RI.2.8	Cross checking... Do the pictures and/or words look right? Do they sound right? Do they make sense? RI.2.4	Reread text RF.2.4	Use prior knowledge and context to predict and confirm meaning RI.2.4
Make a picture or mental image RI.2.7	Flip the sound RF.2.3	Practice common sight words and high-frequency words RF.2.3	Use pictures, illustrations, and diagrams L.2.4
Monitor and fix up: check for understanding /back up and reread RF.2.4	Use the pictures... Do the words and pictures match? RI.2.7	Adjust and apply different reading rates to match text RL.2.6, RF.2.4	Use word parts to determine the meaning of words (prefixes, suffixes, origins, abbreviations, etc.) RF.2.3, L.2.4
Ask questions throughout the reading process RL.2.1, RI.2.1, SL.2.3	Use beginning and ending sounds RF.2.3	Use punctuation to enhance phrasing and prosody (end marks, commas, etc.) L.2.2	Ask someone to define the word for you L.2.6
Use text features (titles, headings, captions, graphic features) RI.2.5	Blend sounds; stretch and reread RF.2.3	Read text as the author would say it, conveying the meaning or feeling RL.2.6	Use dictionaries, thesauruses, and glossaries as tools L.2.2
Summarize text; include sequence of main events RL.2.5, RI.2.2	Chunk letters and sounds together RF.2.3		
Use main idea and supporting details to determine importance RL.2.2	Skip the word, then come back RF.2.4		
Determine and analyze author's purpose and support with text RL.2.6, RI.2.8	Trade a word/guess a word that makes sense RF.2.4		
Recognize literary elements (genre, plot, character, setting, problem/resolution, theme) RL.2.3, RL.2.7	Recognize words at sight RF.2.3		
Recognize and explain cause-and-effect relationships RI.2.3			
Compare and contrast within and between text RL.2.9, RI.2.9			

*Not all Common Core Standards are included in the CAFE Menu, such as writing, speaking, listening, and various other standards.

Ready Reference Guide

A Ready Reference Guide is a one-page download that gives you the most important information to remember when introducing a strategy from the CAFE Menu.

GOAL **COMPREHENSION**	STRATEGY **CHECK FOR UNDERSTANDING**
DEFINITION	A comprehension strategy that teaches children to stop frequently and check, or monitor, whether they understand what they are reading. This typically is a quick summary of what they've read, starting with "who" and "what."
WHY CHILDREN NEED THIS STRATEGY	Often as beginning readers, children are so aware of reading accurately that they forget to take time to think about what they are reading, checking to see whether they understand the text. Advanced readers can develop the habit of reading through text without monitoring even if they were aware of the Check for understanding strategy as beginning readers.
SECRET TO SUCCESS	Knowing when we read that we must think about the story and realize what the author is trying to tell us or what we are learning from the book. Readers stop frequently to check for understanding or to ask who and what.
HOW WE TEACH IT	This vital strategy is not only one of the first we introduce, but also one we model each and every day of the school year. ▪ Modeling during our read-aloud, we stop periodically and say, "Let me see if I remember what I just read. I am going to start by thinking of who the story was about and what happened." ▪ We continue to stop periodically and talk through the "who" and "what," usually about three or four times during each read-aloud. ▪ After modeling this two or three times for students, we start asking them to answer the "who" and the "what" through "listen and talk," asking one student to do it for the whole class and then expecting children to do it on their own. Language we use: "Stop often to check for understanding before you read any farther." "Who did you just read about and what just happened?" "How often did you stop to check for understanding? After each sentence, after each paragraph, at the end of each page?" "Was your brain talking to you while you read?" "Are you finding you are understanding what you are reading?" "What do you do if you don't remember?"
TROUBLESHOOTING	We had a parent cut out large check marks, approximately 7 inches long, from balsa wood. Often we provide these check marks to students as a reminder to stop and check for understanding. They work particularly well when partners are reading together and working on Check for understanding. The person listening to his or her partner read has the job of holding the check mark. When the reader comes to the end of a page or paragraph, the check-mark holder checks for understanding what the reader just read. On one side of the check marks we write, "Check for understanding" and on the other side, "Who and what."

STARTING OUT

CAFE OVERVIEW

CAFE MENU

ACCOUNTABILITY

CAFE SYSTEM

CAFE RESOURCES

RESOURCES

REFLECTION

Curriculum Calendar: Whole-Group Instruction

MONTH:

	WEEK 1	WEEK 2	WEEK 3	WEEK 4
COMPREHENSION SKILL				
COMPREHENSION STRATEGY				
PHONICS				
ACCURACY				
FLUENCY				
WRITING				
MATH				

Reflection . . .

Curriculum Calendar: Whole-Group Instruction

MONTH:

	WEEK 1	WEEK 2	WEEK 3	WEEK 4
COMPREHENSION SKILL	**Understand story elements** ▪ Describe physical traits of characters and tell how they act. ▪ Retell the important events of a story. ▪ Describe the setting of a story. ▪ Identify the speaker/narrator in a story.	**Understand story elements** ▪ Describe physical traits of characters and tell how they act. ▪ Retell the important events of a story. ▪ Describe the setting of a story. ▪ Identify the speaker/narrator in a story.	**Understand story elements** ▪ Describe physical traits of characters and tell how they act. ▪ Retell the important events of a story. ▪ Describe the setting of a story. ▪ Identify the speaker/narrator in a story.	▪ Organize summary information from informational/expository text and/or literary/narrative text into a teacher-provided graphic organizer to enhance text comprehension. Summarize the text.
COMPREHENSION STRATEGY	▪ Identify the main idea of informational/expository passage and support with text-based evidence with teacher guidance.	▪ Identify the main idea of informational/expository passage and support with text-based evidence with teacher guidance.	▪ Identify the main idea of informational/expository passage and support with text-based evidence with teacher guidance.	Author's Viewpoint (not until third grade)
PHONICS	/a/ -afe, -ave, -aze	/ou/ -ound, -ow, -own		
ACCURACY	Reread to clarify the meaning of the word.	Reread to clarify the meaning of the word.	Use prefixes, suffixes, and abbreviations to determine the meaning of the word.	Use prefixes, suffixes, and abbreviations to determine the meaning of the word.
FLUENCY	Reread to make it smooth.	Reread to make it smooth.	I read, you read the same words.	I read, you read the same words.
WRITING	Interview Questions	Interview Questions	Interview Questions	Interview Questions
MATH Lessons: 10.9–11.10	Game: Multiplication Draw		Game: Beat the Calculator	

Whole-Group and Small-Group Planning at a Glance

When assessing your students using the 7 Steps from Assessment to Instruction, record the student's individual strategy or strategies you will be starting with in your CCPensieve, and then mark those strategies in the child's corresponding box on the spreadsheet.

When finished assessing the whole group, you can see other students who have the same goal, which would make for a natural small group, providing curricular coherence across small-group and individual instruction. If you notice a multitude of students all needing the same strategy, this would be a good strategy to teach in the whole group.

	Check for understanding	Back up and reread	Use prior knowledge to connect with text	Make and adjust predictions (use text to confirm)	Infer and support with evidence	Make a picture or mental image	Monitor and fix up	Ask questions throughout the reading process	Use text features (titles, headings, captions, graphic features)	Summarize text; include sequence of main events	Use main ideas and supporting details to determine importance	Determine and analyze author's purpose and support with text	Recognize literary elements	Recognize and explain cause-and-effect relationship	Compare and contrast within and between texts	Abundant easy reading	Look carefully at letters and words	Cross checking (look right, sound right, make sense)	Flip the sound
Genivive																			
Taylor																			
Abjeet																			
Juan																			
Joey																			
Sydney																			
Carlie																			
Benjamin																			
Jaeger																			
Trevor																			
Crystal																			
Ina																			

Reading Level Data

PAPER PENSIEVE

	Independent	Instructional	Frustration		Independent	Instructional	Frustration	GROWTH		Independent	Instructional	Frustration		Independent	Instructional	Frustration	GROWTH

Calendar
PAPER PENSIEVE

JANUARY

*Group

SUN	MON	TUE	WED	THU	FRI	SAT
1	2	3 Kemper Carter Gabrial *Summarize *Cross Check	4 Ava Tessa Torin *Ask Questions *Cross Check	5 Henry Ilona Jessica *Summarize *Cross Check	6 Kemper Rey *Check for Und. *Cross Check	7
8	9 Abigail Evalyn Isaac *Summarize *Check for Und.	10 Ava Reign Fernanda *Tune In	11 Reign Isaac Jessica Rey Fernanda	12 Kemper Marcell *Cross Check *Ask Questions	13 Chelsey Reign *Summarize *Tune In	14
15	16 Ghina Henry Carter *Ask Questions *Tune In	17 Camilla Ayden Reign *Use Text Feat.	18 Isaac Tessa *Check for Und. *Use Text Feat.	19 Chelsey Tessa Marcell Torin Rey Ilona	20 Henry *Tune In *Summarize *Use Text Feat.	21
22	23 Angel Evalyn *Summarize *Use Text Feat.	24 Fernanda *Ask Questions *Cross Check *Check for Und.	25 Kemper Ilona Chelsey *Cross Check	26 Torin *Tune In *Use Text Feat. *Skip Word	27 Carter Abigail *Skip Word *Summarize	28
29	30 Marcell Torin Kemper Camilla Carter	31 Gabrial *Tune In *Use Text Feat. *Cross Check				

Sample

Calendar

CCPENSIEVE.COM

Keeping Track

PAPER PENSIEVE

Abigail	1/4	1/5	1/9	1/10	1/11	1/13	1/16	1/23	1/25	1/27														
Angel	1/4	1/6	1/12	1/17	1/23	1/25	1/30																	
Ava	1/4	1/5	1/10	1/16	1/23	1/26	1/31																	
Ayden	1/3	1/5	1/9	1/10	1/17	1/24	1/27																	
Camilla	1/4	1/6	1/12	1/17	1/23	1/25	1/30																	
Carter	1/3	1/5	1/9	1/10	1/11	1/13	1/16	1/18	1/20	1/24	1/25	1/26	1/27	1/30	1/31									
Chelsey	1/4	1/9	1/13	1/17	1/19	1/24	1/25	1/30																
Evalyn	1/4	1/9	1/16	1/23	1/27	1/31																		
Gabrial	1/3	1/5	1/10	1/16	1/23	1/27	1/31																	
Ghina	1/4	1/6	1/12	1/16	1/23	1/25	1/31																	
Henry	1/3	1/5	1/10	1/16	1/20	1/24	1/27																	
Ilona	1/4	1/5	1/9	1/17	1/19	1/24	1/26	1/31																
Isaac	1/3	1/6	1/9	1/10	1/11	1/13	1/16	1/18	1/20	1/24	1/26	1/27	1/30	1/31										
Jessica	1/5	1/6	1/11	1/16	1/20	1/26	1/30																	
Kemper	1/3	1/5	1/6	1/9	1/10	1/11	1/12	1/13	1/16	1/18	1/20	1/24	1/25	1/26	1/27	1/30	1/31							
Reign	1/4	1/6	1/9	1/10	1/11	1/13	1/16	1/17	1/18	1/20	1/24	1/25	1/26	1/27	1/30	1/31								
Rey	1/3	1/5	1/6	1/11	1/18	1/19	1/24	1/30																
Tessa	1/4	1/5	1/11	1/16	1/18	1/23	1/26	1/30																
Fernanda	1/4	1/6	1/10	1/11	1/20	1/24	1/30																	
Marcell	1/3	1/5	1/10	1/12	1/19	1/23	1/27	1/30																
Torin	1/4	1/6	1/11	1/17	1/19	1/23	1/26	1/30																

Keeping Track

Reading | Writing | Word Work | Math | Science | Social Studies | Other

Students	1	2	3	4	5	6	7	8	9	10	11	12	13	14
Abigail	Jan 4	Jan 5	Jan 9	Jan 10	Jan 11	Jan 13	Jan 16	Jan 23	Jan 25	Jan 27				
Angel	Jan 4	Jan 6	Jan 12	Jan 17	Jan 23	Jan 25	Jan 30							
Ava	Jan 4	Jan 5	Jan 10	Jan 16	Jan 23	Jan 26	Jan 31							
Ayden	Jan 3	Jan 5	Jan 9	Jan 10	Jan 17	Jan 24	Jan 27							
Camilla	Jan 4	Jan 6	Jan 12	Jan 17	Jan 23	Jan 25	Jan 30							
Carter	Jan 3	Jan 5	Jan 9	Jan 10	Jan 11	Jan 13	Jan 16	Jan 18	Jan 20	Jan 24	Jan 25	Jan 26	Jan 27	Jan 30
Chelsey	Jan 4	Jan 9	Jan 13	Jan 17	Jan 19	Jan 24	Jan 25	Jan 30						
Evalyn	Jan 4	Jan 9	Jan 16	Jan 23	Jan 27	Jan 31								
Fernanda	Jan 4	Jan 5	Jan 10	Jan 11	Jan 20	Jan 24	Jan 30							
Gabrial	Jan 3	Jan 6	Jan 10	Jan 16	Jan 23	Jan 27	Jan 31							
Ghina	Jan 4	Jan 6	Jan 12	Jan 16	Jan 23	Jan 25	Jan 31							
Henry	Jan 3	Jan 5	Jan 10	Jan 16	Jan 20	Jan 24	Jan 27							
Ilona	Jan 4	Jan 5	Jan 9	Jan 17	Jan 19	Jan 24	Jan 25	Jan 31						
Isaac	Jan 3	Jan 6	Jan 9	Jan 10	Jan 11	Jan 13	Jan 16	Jan 18	Jan 20	Jan 24	Jan 26	Jan 27	Jan 30	Jan 31
Jessica	Jan 5	Jan 6	Jan 11	Jan 16	Jan 20	Jan 26	Jan 30							
Kemper	Jan 9	Jan 10	Jan 11	Jan 12	Jan 13	Jan 16	Jan 18	Jan 20	Jan 24	Jan 15	Jan 26	Jan 27	Jan 30	Jan 31
Marcell	Jan 3	Jan 5	Jan 10	Jan 12	Jan 19	Jan 23	Jan 27	Jan 30						
Reign	Jan 9	Jan 10	Jan 11	Jan 13	Jan 16	Jan 17	Jan 18	Jan 20	Jan 24	Jan 25	Jan 26	Jan 27	Jan 30	Jan 31
Rey	Jan 3	Jan 5	Jan 6	Jan 11	Jan 18	Jan 19	Jan 24	Jan 30						
Tessa	Jan 4	Jan 5	Jan 11	Jan 16	Jan 18	Jan 23	Jan 26	Jan 30						
Torin	Jan 4	Jan 6	Jan 11	Jan 17	Jan 19	Jan 23	Jan 26	Jan 30						
Groups														
Ask Questions Ilona, Rey	Jan 4	Jan 12	Jan 16	Jan 24										
Check for Understanding Ghina, Marcell, Torin, Ava	Jan 6	Jan 9	Jan 18	Jan 24										
Cross Check Carter, Chelsey, Reign	Jan 3	Jan 4	Jan 5	Jan 6	Jan 12	Jan 24	Jan 25	Jan 31						
Skip Word-Come Back Evalyn, Fernanda, Isaac	Jan 26	Jan 27												
Summarize Abigail, Isaac, Kemper	Jan 3	Jan 5	Jan 9	Jan 13	Jan 20	Jan 23	Jan 27							
Tune In To Interesting Words Gabrial, Henry, Angel, Ayden	Jan 10	Jan 13	Jan 16	Jan 20	Jan 26	Jan 31								
Use Text Features Camilla, Kemper, Reign	Jan 17	Jan 18	Jan 20	Jan 23	Jan 26	Jan 31								

Bold: Added by You

Individual Reading Conferring Sheet

PAPER PENSIEVE

NAME ______________________________

GOALS

-
-

STRENGTHS

-
-

	OBSERVATION AND INSTRUCTION	NEXT STEPS TO MEET GOAL
DATE TOUCH POINT		
DATE TOUCH POINT		
DATE TOUCH POINT		
DATE TOUCH POINT		
DATE TOUCH POINT		
DATE TOUCH POINT		

Individual Reading Conferring Sheet

PAPER PENSIEVE

NAME Kirsten

GOALS Comprehension

- Check for Understanding
-

STRENGTHS

- Fluency
-

	OBSERVATION AND INSTRUCTION	NEXT STEPS TO MEET GOAL
DATE 11/4 TOUCH POINT 1	Danny Goes to the Park continues to read—doesn't stop Practice and model secret practices 2 times together	Partner-read with Micah Stop and check together Meet tomorrow
DATE 11/5 TOUCH POINT 2	Danny's Red Shoes Was aware to stop—and do secret. Think aloud... Here is what you did... Continue to practice	Partner-read seems to be helping Meet with Micah Meet in 2 days
DATE 11/7 TOUCH POINT 3	Danny's Cape Stopped at end of each page. Could say who and what. Identified what she did.	Partner-read Meet in 2 days
DATE 11/11 TOUCH POINT 2	Geologist Danny Read quickly—no stopping Offered advice—stop Could ✓ for understanding with prompting	Add stickies to each page—reminder to stop Meet tomorrow
DATE 11/12 TOUCH POINT 3	Get Down Danny Stopped often—remembers who and what stickies helped her remember	Continue stickies Meet in 2 days
DATE 11/14 TOUCH POINT 3	Danny's Red Socks Stops often— Add a harder book—	Take away stickies Meet in 2 days

NEW TO ME — HAVE QUESTIONS — GOT IT — APPLYING

Student Reading Conferring Sheet

PAPER PENSIEVE

NAME ______________________________

My Goal:
My Strategy:

My Goal:
My Strategy:

My Strengths:

What I may work on next:

	NEXT STEPS TO MEET GOAL		NEXT STEPS TO MEET GOAL
DATE TOUCH POINT		DATE TOUCH POINT	
DATE TOUCH POINT		DATE TOUCH POINT	
DATE TOUCH POINT		DATE TOUCH POINT	
DATE TOUCH POINT		DATE TOUCH POINT	
DATE TOUCH POINT		DATE TOUCH POINT	
DATE TOUCH POINT		DATE TOUCH POINT	

Instructional Protocol Icon Definitions

RECORD SELECTION TITLE

Jot down the title of the selection and page number.

OBSERVE THE STUDENT(S)

Record what the student is doing related to the goal.

THINK ABOUT CONFERENCE FOCUS

Think . . . Do I teach or reinforce what we planned yesterday? Or change the plan based on what I see today? Record what was taught.

RECORD TWO TARGETED GOALS

Record two targets for the student to work on before the next meeting. First goal relates to comprehension. Second is to practice strategy.

DISCUSS NEXT MEETING

Plan next meeting. Record on Pensieve calendar.

Individual Reading Conferring Sheet

WITH ICONS, PAPER PENSIEVE

NAME ____

GOALS

-
-

STRENGTHS

-
-

	OBSERVATION AND INSTRUCTION	NEXT STEPS TO MEET GOAL
DATE TOUCH POINT		Next
DATE TOUCH POINT		Next
DATE TOUCH POINT		Next
DATE TOUCH POINT		Next
DATE TOUCH POINT		Next
DATE TOUCH POINT		Next

Individual Reading Conferring Sheet

WITH ICONS, PAPER PENSIEVE

NAME Jennie

GOALS

- Accuracy—Chunk Sounds and Letters Together
- Next strategy—Flip the Sound?

STRENGTHS

- Listening Comprehension
-

	OBSERVATION AND INSTRUCTION	NEXT STEPS TO MEET GOAL
DATE TOUCH POINT	Mr. Whisper Chunked 2 words Worked on blends—bl, gr	1. Comprehension—think 2. Practice blending sounds—bl, gr Next: Check beginning blends
DATE TOUCH POINT	The Wind Blows Strong Has beginning blends (onset) Missing ending blends (rime) Focus on ending blend spl osh	1. Check for understanding 2. Sticky words with ending chunk Next: Check rimes!
DATE TOUCH POINT	The Secret of Spooky House Read "spooky"—wow Stickied 3 words Starting to see chunks Reviewed and practiced chunks	1. Think 2. Continue to sticky Next: Watch for vowel sounds
DATE TOUCH POINT	The Secret of Spooky House Stickied 3 words Start to phase out instruction	1. Retell 2. Think about chunks and when it works Next: Appointment in 3 days Think about flip sounds
DATE TOUCH POINT		Next
DATE TOUCH POINT		Next

Strategy Group Instruction Sheet

PAPER PENSIEVE

GOAL	STRATEGY	NAMES	TOUCH POINTS	INDIVIDUAL CONFERRING TOUCH POINTS
DATE	LESSON			

GOAL	STRATEGY			
DATE	LESSON			

GOAL	STRATEGY			
DATE	LESSON			

Strategy Group Instruction Sheet

PAPER PENSIEVE

GOAL Comprehension	STRATEGY Check for Understanding	NAMES	TOUCH POINTS	INDIVIDUAL CONFERRING TOUCH POINTS
DATE	LESSON			
11/4	Introduce Strategy and Secret Model with Incredible Life of Riley—3 times Students practice in own books Review strategy—Kirsten modeled Assign—practice strategy in own book Meet tomorrow	Quinton Lena Micha	2,3,3 1,2,2	
11/5	Observe—review strategy Each student read 1 sentence and model strategy Review—assign sticky notes Meet tomorrow	Kirsten	1-2,2,2	1,2,3,2
11/6	Review and model each practice—meet 2 days			

GOAL	STRATEGY			
DATE	LESSON			

GOAL	STRATEGY			
DATE	LESSON			

NEW TO ME — HAVE QUESTIONS — GOT IT — APPLYING

Understanding Touch Points

QUANTIFYING OUR WORK WITH STUDENTS

Our scoring system is based on Touch Points instead of quizzes and tests. Every time we touch base with a student—in a small group and one-on-one—we take notes and score their proficiency.

- **4 Exceeding Standard**
- **3 Meeting Standard**
- **2 Approaching Standard**
- **1 Below Standard**

For example, if a student needs Check for understanding to enhance comprehension, we introduce the strategy and put a 1 (for below standard) in the space under "Touch Point" on the student's conferring form. The next time we meet with them, we give them a score to reflect their proficiency.

Once a child receives four or five 3s or 4s in a row, we trust they have competently added the strategy to the repertoire of strategies they have control of, and we layer on a new strategy to their instruction. Though we phase out direct instruction, we continue to monitor the strategy use periodically. So when you touch base, think Touch Point. It's a great way to monitor progress toward a goal.

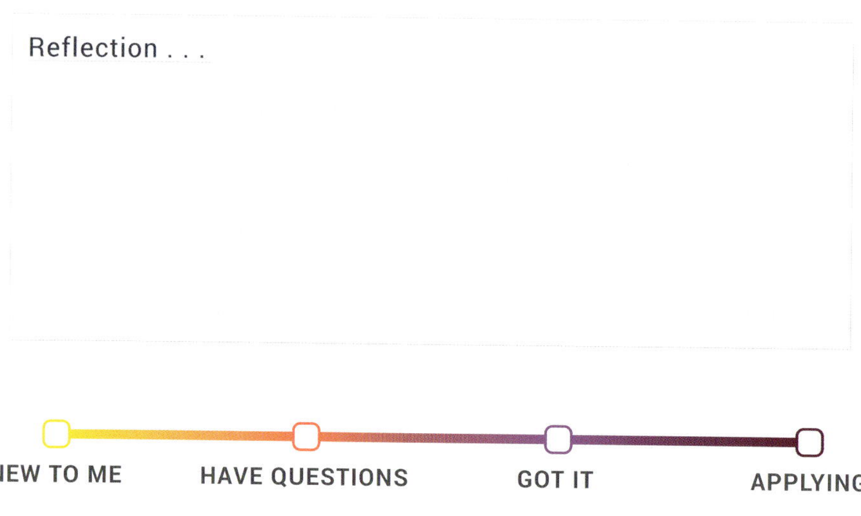

Touch Points

Touch Points monitor teaching and document student learning.

4 Exceeding Standard

3 Meeting Standard

2 Approaching Standard

1 Below Standard

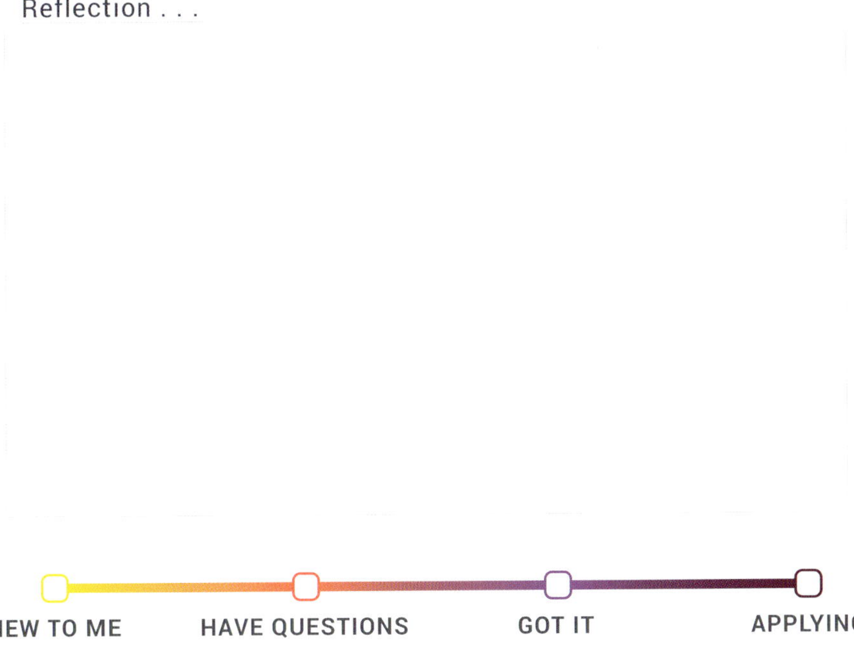

In 3 teaching attempts, if student gets 1's or 2's as Touch Points

CHANGE SOMETHING

MATERIALS

- Fiction
- Nonfiction
- Reading Level

SETTING

- One-on-One
- Small Group

TEACHING

- Explicit Explanation
- Model
- Think Aloud
- Offer Advice

NEW TO ME — HAVE QUESTIONS — GOT IT — APPLYING

Progress Monitoring
of Teaching and Learning (continued)

In 4 or 5 observations, if student gets 3's or 4's as Touch Points

LAYER ON A NEW STRATEGY

CAFE SYSTEM

Structure of Daily 5 and CAFE

	SESSION 1		SESSION 2		SESSION 3	
Focus Lesson—Content 7–10 minutes	**DAILY 5 STUDENT CHOICES** Read to Self Read to Someone Listen to Reading Work on Writing Word Work **CAFE TEACHER CHOICES** Individual Conferring Guided Groups Assessing 1–2 Small Group(s) and/or 3–4 Individual Conferences	Focus Lesson—Content 7–10 minutes	**DAILY 5 STUDENT CHOICES** Read to Self Read to Someone Listen to Reading Work on Writing Word Work **CAFE TEACHER CHOICES** Individual Conferring Guided Groups Assessing 1–2 Small Group(s) and/or 3–4 Individual Conferences	Focus Lesson—Content 7–10 minutes	**DAILY 5 STUDENT CHOICES** Read to Self Read to Someone Listen to Reading Work on Writing Word Work **CAFE TEACHER CHOICES** Individual Conferring Guided Groups Assessing 1–2 Small Group(s) and/or 3–4 Individual Conferences	Review Focus Lessons—Content & Share 7–10 minutes

Reflection . . .

NEW TO ME — HAVE QUESTIONS — GOT IT — APPLYING

7 Steps from Assessment to Instruction

1. **Assess individual student**
2. **Review assessments and identify potential goals and strategies**
3. **Discuss with student, set goal and strategy**
4. **Student declares goal on the CAFE Menu**
5. **Record goal and strategy on individual conferring sheet**
6. **Record student's name on strategy group form**
7. **Ready for instruction**

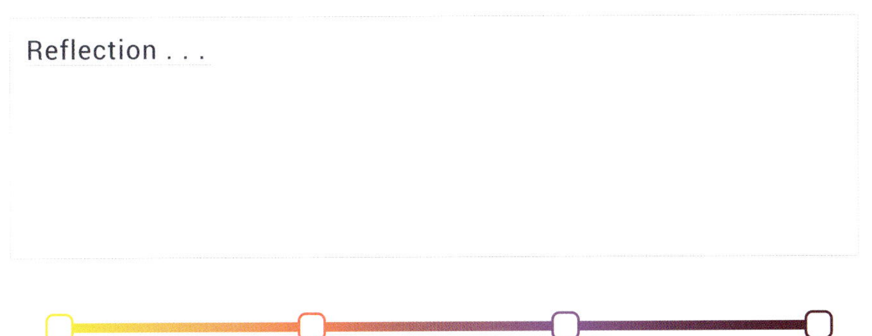

The CAFE Menu 6-5-4-3

CHOOSING THE RIGHT STRATEGY

COMPREHENSION I understand what I read	ACCURACY I can read the words	FLUENCY I can read accurately, with expression, and understand what I read	EXPAND VOCABULARY I know, find, and use interesting words
STRATEGIES	**STRATEGIES**	**STRATEGIES**	**STRATEGIES**
Check for understanding	Abundant easy reading	Voracious reading	Voracious reading
Back up and reread	Look carefully at letters and words	Read appropriate-level texts that are a good fit	Tune in to interesting words and use new vocabulary in speaking and writing
Use prior knowledge to connect with text	Cross checking . . . Do the pictures and/or words look right? Do they sound right? Do they make sense?	Reread text	Use prior knowledge and context to predict and confirm meaning
Make and adjust predictions; use text to confirm	Flip the sound	Practice common sight words and high-frequency words	Use pictures, illustrations, and diagrams
Infer and support with evidence	Use the pictures . . . Do the words and pictures match?	Adjust and apply different reading rates to match text	Use word parts to determine the meaning of words (prefixes, suffixes, origins, abbreviations, etc.)
Make a picture or mental image	Use beginning and ending sounds	Use punctuation to enhance phrasing and prosody (end marks, commas, etc.)	Ask someone to define the word for you
Monitor and fix up	Blend sounds; stretch and reread	Read text as the author would say it, conveying the meaning or feeling	Use dictionaries, thesauruses, and glossaries as tools
Ask questions throughout the reading process	Chunk letters and sounds together		
Use text features (titles, headings, captions, graphic features)	Skip the word, then come back		
Summarize text; include sequence of main events	Trade a word/guess a word that makes sense		
Use main idea and supporting details to determine importance	Recognize words at sight		
Determine and analyze author's purpose and support with text			
Recognize literary elements (genre, plot, character, setting, problem/resolution, theme)			
Recognize and explain cause-and-effect relationships			
Compare and contrast within and between text			
6	5	4	3

BEHAVIORS THAT SUPPORT READING

Get started right away | Stay in one spot | Work quietly | Read the whole time | Increase stamina | Ignore distractions | Persevere

Reflection . . .

NEW TO ME — HAVE QUESTIONS — GOT IT — APPLYING

From Assessment to Conferring

WHAT WE ARE SEEING	POTENTIAL GOALS	POSSIBLE STRATEGY	ALTERNATIVE STRATEGY
Student jumps right into reading story, then lacks understanding	Comprehension	Use prior knowledge to connect with text	Ask questions while reading, Back up and reread
Doesn't remember details but understands the main idea	Comprehension	Retell the story	Recognize literary elements
Doesn't remember details from nonfiction	Comprehension	Use text features (titles, headings, captions, graphic features)	Determine and analyze author's purpose and support with text
Can't remember what was read	Comprehension	Check for understanding	Retell or summarize, Make a picture or mental image, Determine importance using theme, main ideas, and supporting details
Can comprehend literally but can't read between the lines	Comprehension	Infer and support with evidence	Ask questions while reading, Predict what will happen; use text to confirm
Leaving off ends of words	Accuracy	Cross checking	Chunk letters together
Stalls on words	Accuracy	Skip the word, then come back	Blend sounds; stretch and reread
Reads words with correct letters but wrong sounds	Accuracy	Flip the sound	Cross checking
Sounds out each individual letter	Accuracy	Chunk letters together, Cross checking	Blend sounds
Reading too quickly	Fluency	Adjust and apply different reading rates to match text	Use punctuation to enhance phrasing and prosody
Chooses books that are too hard	Reading Behaviors Book Selection	I PICK	Read first chapters to student
Doesn't stick with a book	Reading Behaviors Book Selection	Read appropriate-level text, Choose good-fit books	Voracious reading

ADD YOUR OWN:

NEW TO ME HAVE QUESTIONS GOT IT APPLYING

Instruction Protocol: Productive, Effective, Focused Teaching and Learning

1 **CHECK** calendar for appointments.

2 **PREPARE** (30 seconds)

Review your conferring notes for the student's strengths and strategy focus.

3 **OBSERVE** (1 minute)

"[Student], please read so I can listen in; then tell me about yourself as a reader."

Observe the student. Is he or she applying the skill/strategy taught or reinforced last time you met?

What is the student doing well with his or her strategy/skill application?

4 **REINFORCE AND TEACH** (1 minute)

"I noticed ________ ; what did you notice? Today we are going to ________."

Verbally share with student your observations of what he or she was doing well.

Teach or reinforce the skill or strategy you think is just right for the student now by

- explicit explanation,
- modeling,
- thinking aloud, and
- offering advice.

5 **PRACTICE** (1 minute)

"Now it is your turn. You try..."

Ask the student to practice the skill/strategy while you listen in.

6 **PLAN** (30 seconds)

"This is what I am hearing, and because of that, this may be our next step."

Next

Based on today's teaching and learning, decide and agree together what the next step will be. It isn't uncommon for students to need continued practice with the previous strategy.

Write this plan on the coaching sheet.

7 **ENCOURAGE** (15 seconds)

Just before you leave the student, encourage him or her to continue to practice the skill taught or reinforced today.

Student should articulate the goal.

NOTES

- The times above serve as guidelines, and though it isn't necessary to strictly adhere to them, they will give you a general idea so you can keep your conferences focused and brief.
- Each step above may be shorter or longer, depending on what the child is doing that day, and where you are in the gradual release of teaching the skills or strategies to the student.
- Remember that brief, focused conferences that occur frequently are considerably more beneficial than sporadic, lengthy ones.

NEW TO ME HAVE QUESTIONS GOT IT APPLYING

STARTING OUT

CAFE OVERVIEW

CAFE MENU

ACCOUNTABILITY

CAFE SYSTEM

CAFE RESOURCES

RESOURCES

REFLECTION

Parent Pipeline

By Allison Behne

Parent Pipelines are guides to help parents assist their children with their goals and strategies at home. We do not send every Parent Pipeline home with each child, just the one that is directly linked to what they are working on in the classroom. It is one more way to provide individualized instruction to each and every child, giving them what they need to help make them successful.

CAFE GOAL	CAFE STRATEGY
COMPREHENSION	**CHECK FOR UNDERSTANDING**

Even as an adult reader, there are times when I am reading a story, get lost, and am not sure what has happened. Fortunately, when this happens, I have strategies to help me understand the story. The same thing happens when children read. However, children often keep reading and do not realize they have lost comprehension until the end of the story. They are too concerned with reading accurately, and forget to take the time to think about what they are reading. How can we help them gain comprehension? We can teach them the comprehension strategy Check for understanding, because good readers stop frequently to check for understanding or to ask who and what.

How can you help your child with this strategy at home?

1. When reading to your child, stop periodically and say, "Let's see if we remember what I just read. Think about who the story was about and what happened." Do this three or four times throughout the story.

2. When reading to your child, stop and have them practice checking for understanding by saying, "I heard you say..."

3. Ask your child the following questions:
    - Who did you just read about?
    - What just happened?
    - Was your brain talking to you while you read?
    - Do you understand what was read?
    - What do you do if you don't remember?

Thank you for your continued support at home!

NEW TO ME — HAVE QUESTIONS — GOT IT — APPLYING

Leadership Support: Show the Research

School administrators often write to ask how they can support their teachers in implementing Daily 5 and CAFE successfully. Similarly, teachers often write to ask how they can get their district to "allow" or "support" them in their quest to implement Daily 5/CAFE in their classroom. Many districts and teachers are seeing great things happen in their Daily 5/CAFE classrooms and are encouraging others to read and implement Daily 5 and CAFE. Some districts have seen such a positive effect that it has become a district-wide initiative. School leaders understand the importance of implementing a program/idea with fidelity and want to support their teachers. The question is... HOW? We hope to provide some assistance to administrators through a series of articles touching on some fundamental ways to support teachers. We begin with a support suggestion that is essential to creating teacher and district "buy-in."

ADMINISTRATIVE SUPPORT SUGGESTION #1: SHOW THE RESEARCH!

One of the foundational principles essential to the Daily 5 is "creating a sense of urgency" (Boushey & Moser, 2006). Teaching students why we do something gives them a purpose and helps them understand the reasons they are putting forth the effort to learn something new. It assists students in accepting responsibility and ownership of their learning. This really is no different for adults. When given a plausible reason for a task, adults often become motivated to complete the task. Therefore, when looking to introduce a staff or district to Daily 5/CAFE, it is important to create a sense of urgency and provide them with the "why." The best way to do this is by showing them the research!

Daily 5 (Boushey & Moser, 2006) and CAFE (Boushey & Moser, 2009) are based on current research in teaching and learning. The foundational principles, routines, and concepts of both Daily 5 and CAFE are supported by researchers such as Richard Allington, Margaret Mooney, Nancie Atwell, Michael Pressley, Ken Wesson, David Pearson, Regie Routman, Emmett Betts, Michael Grinder, Peter Johnston, Doug Fisher, Nancy Frey, Robert Marzano, and the list goes on. Many schools conduct informal action research projects on both Daily 5 and CAFE, and a few formal studies are in the process of being conducted. Below are a few highlights of research that will provide good discussion and help create the sense of urgency needed to motivate teachers and districts to make the leap into the Daily 5/CAFE approach to literacy instruction.

> Skilled teachers use instructional scaffolds, such as posing questions to check for understanding, during small-group guided instruction (Frey & Fisher, 2010). Daily 5 sets up a classroom for effective small-group instruction to take place. CAFE provides an organizational tool and a menu of strategies for teachers to use in developing and implementing strategy group instruction.

Leadership Support: Show the Research *(continued)*

One way to teach our students to be independent learners is to gradually transfer the responsibility for learning to them (Fisher & Frey, 2008). In Daily 5, students gradually build stamina until they are successful at working independently on their reading and writing tasks.

Allowing children to choose their own books will encourage a love of reading (Atwell, 2007). Good-fit books are an essential component of Daily 5, and through a series of mini-lessons, students learn how to choose good-fit books for their book boxes.

Clear expectations and learning goals reduce student misbehavior and help create a positive learning environment (R. Marzano & J. Marzano, 2003). The use of I-charts in Daily 5 allows students to develop classroom expectations during the literacy block. A list of behaviors is created, modeled, and reviewed daily until students have mastered the expectations. The chart is posted in the classroom at all times, anchoring their learning to it. In Daily 5, students know what is expected of them and can spend their time focused on learning.

Allington (2012) highlights the importance of self-selected text that a student can read with 98 percent accuracy. He says students must read something they understand that is personally meaningful. In Daily 5/CAFE, students select books that follow the "I-PICK" guidelines. Students are reading good-fit books of their choice and writing about topics that are of interest to them.

Effective assessment that informs instruction matters (Johnston, 2011). The CAFE system allows a teacher to make meaning of student assessment data by organizing results and categorizing students by strategy needs. Through the use of a conferring notebook, teachers have individualized information on each child and can truly design instruction around each child's specific needs.

The amount of research to support the ideas, concepts, and foundational pieces of both Daily 5 and CAFE is abundant. If your school is focused on RTI, differentiated instruction, formative/summative assessment, brain research, co-teaching, student-centered learning, or even best practices in teaching and learning, then Daily 5 and CAFE will prove to be a good fit. To find actual student data that supports the efforts of beginning Daily 5 and CAFE, visit the discussion board on TheDailyCAFE.com, and talk with other educators who are

Leadership Support: Show the Research *(continued)*

using it in their classroom. Informal action research is continually going on in schools all over the world, and teachers are usually more than willing to share their results.

If you are looking to spark curiosity or "create a sense of urgency" with your staff/district/colleagues, ask the following question: How would you like to have a classroom of independent readers and writers, where each student has individual goals and you have time to work with small groups and confer with students individually each day? They may not believe it is possible, but it is, and this thought should certainly spark their curiosity. Present the research that we know is true about reading, writing, and literacy instruction. Then, provide an opportunity for them to really let it sink in. Effective educators do what's best for kids, and consistently strive to make a difference. After viewing, discussing, and understanding the research, the sense of urgency will be established and the true work can begin.

EVEN FURTHER READING

Read the other two articles in this three-part series at TheDailyCAFE.com by searching for the titles below.

Leadership Support: The Gift of Time *(Part 2 of 3)*

Allison Behne provides administrators with two ways instructional leaders can support the teachers who are implementing Daily 5 in their classrooms.

Leadership Support: Know What to Look For *(Part 3 of 3)*

Administrators wanting to support their teachers often want to know what to look for when they go into the classroom. What indicates that Daily 5 and CAFE are being used? Here are a few ideas.

Lit Lesson

Lit Lessons provide a short synopsis of a children's book and a few possible strengths for strategy instruction and teaching possibilities. Visit the TheDailyCAFE.com for an ever-growing collection of 85+ Lit Lessons.

A BAD CASE OF STRIPES
BY DAVID SHANNON

Camilla is out to impress all of her friends, and because of this she is embarrassed to admit that she loves lima beans. Everything is fine until one day Camilla gets a case of the stripes . . . a BAD case of the stripes. Will she learn to be true to herself?

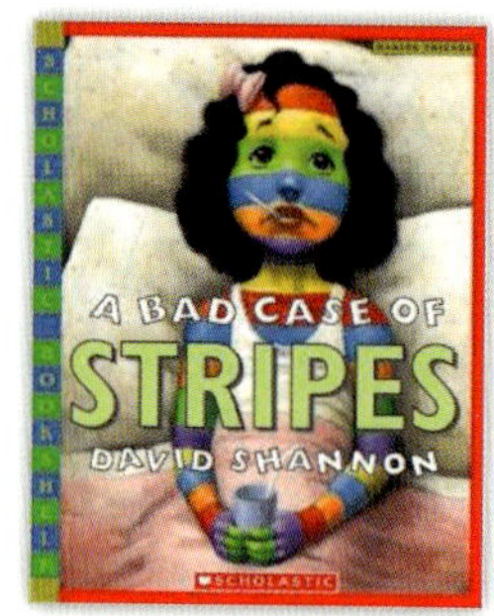

POSSIBLE STRATEGIES FOR INSTRUCTION:

COMPREHENSION

Predict what will happen; use text to confirm

- Use this strategy to assist students in making connections and becoming engaged in the text. There are many places in this text that encourage readers to think ahead. Remember to revisit predictions and use text to confirm.
  - After reading p. 1, ask students why they think Camilla screamed.
  - On p. 2, confirm and adjust predictions, and make a new prediction about why Camilla is covered in stripes.
  - P. 4: Ask students to predict what will happen when Camilla goes to school.
  - After reading p. 13, ask what will happen when Camilla takes her medicine.
  - After p. 24, predict what the old woman will do to help.

Determine and analyze author's purpose and support with text

- Ask students, "In writing this story, was the author's purpose to entertain, inform, or persuade?" What text from the story supports their conclusion?
- Many times, authors have more than one purpose in writing a story. Although the main purpose of this story is to entertain, see if students are able to find any addition underlying purposes. (The overall message of the story about being true to yourself might be one idea a student could present.)

Make a picture or mental image

- This story is perfect to use in teaching visualization! Read each page aloud without showing pictures to allow students to visualize what is happening (you may even want to provide a short pause for students to draw what they visualize). After providing "think time," reveal the photos in the text.

Lit Lesson
(continued)

ACCURACY

Skip the word, then come back

- Before reading, select a few words in the text to cover up. While reading the text, model this strategy by skipping over the covered word and reading the rest of the sentence. Then, return to the sentence, viewing only the first letter of the covered word. Using the first letter and the context of the sentence, try to figure out the word. This strategy will work with many words in this text. Here are a few to try:
  - p. 1—quite
  - p. 4—drowsiness
  - p. 10—contagious
  - p. 16—authority
  - p. 18— bizarre

FLUENCY

Use punctuation to enhance phrasing and prosody

- This text provides many opportunities to use intonation when reading. When using this strategy, think aloud and tell your students to notice the up and down of your voice. Explain to them why your tone changes as you read a question versus a statement.
  - p. 2—"Oh my heavens! You're completely covered with stripes!"
  - p. 2—"Do you feel all right?"
  - p. 8—"Let's see some purple polka dots!"
  - p. 22—"What are we going to do? It just keeps getting worse and worse!"
  - p. 26—"Yuck! No one likes lima beans, especially me!"

Read the text as the author would say it, conveying the meaning or feeling

- This strategy goes hand in hand with using punctuation to enhance phrasing and prosody. As you explain to students how to use intonation when reading, model the difference between reading in a monotone and reading with meaning and feeling.

EXPAND VOCABULARY

Tune in to interesting words and use new vocabulary in speaking and writing

- Select two–three words from the text to focus on. Introduce them to students. When coming across them in reading, say them, have students say them, write them, add them to the word collector, and continue to revisit these words daily to provide multiple exposure and enhance comprehension. Possible choices are:
  - fretting, impress, contagious, relieved, uncontrollable, disaster, incredible, and vanished

This text can be used with nearly any strategy on the CAFE Menu. The above strategies are a highlighted collection to use as a springboard for further instruction.

STARTING OUT

CAFE OVERVIEW

CAFE MENU

ACCOUNTABILITY

CAFE SYSTEM

CAFE RESOURCES

RESOURCES

REFLECTION

Get Graduate Credit for This Workshop

Earn one graduate-level professional development credit from Upper Iowa University by participating in one of The 2 Sisters live workshops or online seminars. See the requirements below.

CAN I EARN CLOCK HOURS INSTEAD?

Many states accept credit from regionally accredited two- or four-year colleges at the 100 (freshman) level or above to be used toward maintenance. One semester hour of college credit is the equivalent of 15 clock hours. State licensing departments and school districts vary regarding their criteria for credit acceptance. It is your responsibility to check with your individual state or district.

WHAT IS THE COST PER CREDIT?

- One credit = $75.00
- Two credits = $150.00

WHAT ARE THE REQUIREMENTS?

- Attend a 2 Sisters workshop or online seminar (registration information will be given there).
- Read the online Getting Started guide content that coincides with your workshop.
- Write one two–three-page reflective essay for each credit.
- Within six months of the workshop date, submit registration information, a copy of your workshop attendance certificate, a copy of the grading rubric, and your paper(s) to either
    - daily5papers@uiu.edu or
    - Upper Iowa University Des Moines Center
Daily 5/CAFE Workshop Credit
5000 Westown Pkwy
West Des Moines, Iowa 50266

ARE YOU INTERESTED?

For reflection paper guidelines, paper template, Getting Started guide content, and complete information, visit the URL below.

http://www.thedailycafe.com/articles/workshopseminar-credit

More Professional Development Options

Professional development from The 2 Sisters helps you jump-start and enhance your Daily 5 and CAFE practices so you get better results faster. All classes impart the latest research and takeaways from recent classroom experiences. Our workshops, online seminars, and online graduate course appeal to different learning styles and geographies. Participants tell us they are all confidence-builders.

Here is a breakdown comparison of all our PD opportunities:

	LIVE WORKSHOPS	ONLINE SEMINARS	GRADUATE COURSE
FORMAT	Live	Online	Online
INSTRUCTION FROM	The 2 Sisters	Allison Behne	Allison Behne
LENGTH	1 full day	4 weeks	8 weeks
CONTENT	Each workshop day is specific to Daily 5 + Math Daily 3 or CAFE	Each seminar is specific to Daily 5, Math Daily 3, or CAFE	Courses include instruction in Daily 5 and CAFE or Math Daily 3
CREDIT	Optional 1 graduate credit per day* (extra credit and fee apply)	Optional 1 graduate credit per seminar* (extra credit and fee apply)	3 graduate credits (included)
TRAINING SIZE	Varies depending on location	120 max./seminar	20 max./course
COST	$255/day (credit card) $295/day (check or purchase order)	$149/seminar (credit card only)	$485
WEBSITE MEMBERSHIP	1-month membership to thedailycafe.com **and** ccpensieve.com for attending one or both workshops.	3-month membership to thedailycafe.com included	Participants must purchase minimum of 3-month subscription to thedailycafe.com

Learn more about workshops and seminars: http://www.thedailycafe.com/workshops

Learn more about the graduate course: http://www.uiu.edu/the2sisters

*Graduate credits available: Earn one credit for Daily 5, one for Math Daily 3, and/or one for CAFE in your preferred mode of instruction: live workshop or online seminar.

The Daily CAFE is a resource that is rich in content to help you discover, refine, and refresh your teaching practice and implementation of Daily 5, Math Daily 3, CAFE, and Classroom Design. You'll be able to find what you need, when you need it, in an online format that promotes creative, independent, and successful learning.

Membership provides unlimited access to continuously updated content, articles, lesson plans, videos, book reviews, parent support documents, and some things we hope simply feed your heart.

Every plan includes complete support for all stages of your Daily 5, CAFE, and Math Daily 3 practice—whether you're just starting out or have years of experience. You'll receive the following:

- Unlimited access to over 4,000 resources related to the methods, classroom design, teaching, and student behavior
- Demonstration videos from live classroom situations
- Downloadable forms and materials for classroom use
- New resources—such as articles, lessons, and videos—every week
- Discussion boards for questions and sharing best practices
- Weekly Nugget email to help you get more from your membership

CCPensieve is your portable conferring assistant, an organized place for safekeeping knowledge about each student as you implement the Daily 5 and CAFE strategies for reading and all the subjects you teach.

If organization isn't your "thing," rely on CCPensieve to keep track of student interactions, conferences, commitments, and next steps. For the über-organized, CCPensieve online offers opportunities to analyze and share the knowledge you gain about students with other users, colleagues, planning teams, and administrators.

FEATURES

- Step-by-step tutorials to help you get started
- Self-populating CAFE goals and strategies on conferring form
- Real-time student/strategy group sharing
- Calendar to schedule meetings with students and groups
- Self-populating keeping-track sheet
- Multiple conferring and subject options
- PDF and CSV export and report options
- Interactive CAFE Menu for strategy help, at the ready
- Student archiving and transferring to new teacher
- Weekly Nugget email to help you get more from your membership

Bibliography

Ackerman, Kristin, Jennifer McDonough. 2016. *Conferring with Young Writers: What to Do When You Don't Know What to Do*. Portland, ME: Stenhouse.

Allen, Jennifer. 2016. *Becoming a Literacy Leader.* 2nd ed. Portland, ME: Stenhouse.

Allington, Richard. 2009. *What Really Matters in Response to Intervention: Research-Based Designs*. Boston, MA: Pearson Education.

----------. 2012. *What Really Matters for Struggling Readers: Designing Research-Based Programs*. Boston, MA: Pearson Education.

Allington, Richard, and Rachael Gabriel. 2012. "Every Child, Every Day." *Educational Leadership*, 69(6), 10–15.

Allington, Richard, and Peter Johnston. 2002. *Reading to Learn: Lessons From Exemplary Fourth-Grade Classrooms*. New York: Guilford Press.

Anderson, Richard C., Paul T. Wilson, and Linda C. Fielding. 1988. "Growth in Reading and How Children Spend Their Time Outside of School." *Reading Research Quarterly*, 23, 285–303.

Atwell, Nancie. 2007. "The Pleasure Principle." *Instructor*, 116(5), 44-60.

----------. 2015. *In the Middle: A Lifetime of Learning About Writing, Reading and Adolescents.* 3rd ed. Portsmouth, NH: Heinemann.

Beck, Isabel, Margaret McKeown, and Linda Kucan. 2013. *Bringing Words to Life: Robust Vocabulary Instruction*. New York: Guilford Press.

Benson, Jeffrey. 2014. *Hanging In: strategies for Teaching the Students Who Challenge Us Most*. Alexandria, VA: ASCD.

Betts, Emmett. 1946. *Foundations of Reading Instruction*. New York: American Book Co.

----------. 1949. "Adjusting Instruction to Individual Needs." In *The Fourth-Eighth Yearbook of the National Society for the Study of Education: Part II, Reading in the School*, ed. N. B. Henry. Chicago: University of Chicago Press.

Boaler, Jo. 2015. *Mathematical Mindsets: Unleashing Students' Potential Through Creative Math, Inspiring Messages and Innovative Teaching*. San Francisco, CA: Jossey-Bass.

Boushey, Gail, and Joan Moser. 2009. *The CAFE Book: Engaging All Students in Daily Literacy Assessment and Instruction*. Portland, ME: Stenhouse.

----------. 2009. The Daily CAFE. http://www.thedailycafe.com.

----------. 2012. CAFE Conferring Pensieve. http://www.ccpensieve.com.

----------. 2014. *The Daily Five: Fostering Literacy Independence in the Elementary Grades*. 2nd ed. Portland, ME: Stenhouse.

Burkins, Jan, and Kim Yaris. 2014. *Reading Wellness: Lessons in Independence and Proficiency.* Portland, ME: Stenhouse.

Calkins, Lucy, Mary Ehrenworth, and Christopher Lehman. 2012. *Pathways to the Common Core: Accelerating Achievement*. Portsmouth, NH: Heinemann.

Collins, Kathy, and Matt Glover. 2015. *I Am Reading: Nurturing Young Children's Meaning Making and Joyful Engagement with Any Book.* Portsmouth, NH: Heinemann.

Duffy, Gerald G. 2014. *Explaining Reading: A Resource for Explicitly Teaching of the Common Core Standards.* 3rd ed. New York: Guilford Press.

Farstrup, Alan E., and S. Jay Samuels, eds. 2011. *What Research Has to Say About Reading Instruction*. 4th ed. Newark, DE: International Reading Association.

Fisher, Douglas, and Nancy Frey. 2008. "Releasing Responsibility." *Educational Leadership*, 66(3), 32-37.

Fisher, Douglas, Nancy Frey, and Stefani Arzonetti Hite. 2016. *Intentional and Targeted Teaching: A Framework for Teacher Growth and Leadership.* Alexandria, VA: ASCD.

Bibliography *(continued)*

Fisher, Douglas, Nancy Frey, and John Hattie. 2016. *Visible Learning for Literacy: Implementing the Practices that Work Best to Accelerate Student Learning*. Thousand Oaks, CA: Corwin.

Frey, Nancy, and Douglas Fisher. 2010. "Identifying Instructional Moves During Guided Learning." *Reading Teacher*, 64(2), 84-95. doi:10.1598/RT.64.2.1.

Fletcher, Ralph, and JoAnn Portalupi. 2013, 1993. *What a Writer Needs*. Portland, ME: Stenhouse.

Hattie, John. 2008. *Visible Learning: A Synthesis of Over 800 Meta-Analyses Relating to Achievement*. New York: Routledge.

----------. 2012. *Visible Learning for Teachers: Maximizing Impact on Learning*. New York: Routledge.

Hattie, John, and Gregory Yates. 2013. *Visible Learning and the Science of How We Learn.* New York: Routledge.

Hichman, Kathleen A., and Heather K. Sheridan-Thomas. 2014. *Best Practices in Adolescent Literacy Instruction*. 2nd ed. New York: Guilford Press.

Hulme, Joy. 2005. *Wild Fibonacci: Nature's Secret Code Revealed*. New York: Random House.

Humphreys, Cathy, and Ruth Parker. 2015. *Making Number Talks Matter: Developing Mathematical Practices and Deepening Understanding. Grades 4–10*. Portland, ME: Stenhouse.

Gallagher, Kelly. 2009. *Readicide: How Schools Are Killing Reading and What You Can Do About It*. Portland, ME: Stenhouse.

----------. 2011. *Write Like This: Teaching Real-World Writing Through Modeling & Mentor Texts*. Portland, ME: Stenhouse.

Gambrell, Linda. 2011. "Seven Rules of Engagement: What's Most Important to Know About Motivation to Read." *The Reading Teacher,* 65(3): 172–178.

Goldberg, Gravity. 2015. *Mindsets and Moves: Strategies That Help Readers Take Charge, Grades 1–8* Thousand Oaks, CA: Corwin Press.

Gregory, Gayle, Martha Kaufeldt. 2015. *The Motivated Brain: Improving Student Attention, Engagement, and Perseverance*. Alexandria, VA: ASCD.

Grinder, Michael. 1995. *ENVoY: Your Personal Guide to Classroom Management*. Battle Ground, WA: Michael Grinder and Associates.

Howard, Mary. 2009. *RTI from All Sides: What Every Teacher Needs to Know*. Portsmouth, NH: Heinemann.

Johnston, Peter. 2011. "Response to Intervention in Literacy." *Elementary School Journal*, 111(4): 511–534.

Johnston, Peter, Richard Allington, and Peter Afflerbach. 1985. "The Congruence of Classroom and Remedial Reading Instruction." *Elementary School Journal, 85, 465–478.*

Marten, Cindy. 2003. *Word Crafting: Teaching Spelling, Grades K–6*. Portsmouth, NH: Heinemann.

Marzano, Robert and Jana Marzano. 2003. "The Key to Classroom Management." *Educational Leadership*, 61(1): 6–13.

Medina, John. 2009. *Brain Rules: 12 Principles for Surviving and Thriving at Work, Home and School*. Seattle, WA: Pear Press.

Meigs-Kahlenber, Vicki. 2016. *The Author's Apprentice: Developing Writing Fluency, Stamina, and Motivation Through Authentic Publication*. Portland, ME: Stenhouse.

Miller, Donalyn. 2009. *The Book Whisperer: Awakening the Inner Reader in Every Child*. San Francisco, CA: Jossey-Bass.

----------. 2014. *Reading in the Wild*. San Francisco, CA: Jossey-Bass.

Mooney, Margaret. 1990. *Reading To, With and By Children*. Katonah, NY: Richard C. Owen.

Bibliography
(continued)

Morrow, Lesley Mandel, Linda Gambrell, and Michael Pressley. 2007. *Best Practices in Literacy Instruction*. New York: Guilford Press.

Pressley, Michael, Richard Allington, Ruth Wharton-McDonald, Cathy Collins Block, and Lesley Mandel Morrow. 2001. *Learning to Read: Lessons from Exemplary First-Grade Classrooms*. New York: Guilford Press.

Ray, Katie Wood. 2010. *In Pictures and In Words: Teaching the Qualities of Good Writing Through Illustration Study*. Portsmouth, NH: Heinemann.

Roth, Kate, and Joan Dabrowski. 2016. *Interactive Writing Across Grades: A Small Practice with Big Results, PreK–5*. Portland, ME: Stenhouse.

Routman, Regie. 2003. *Reading Essentials: The Specifics You Need to Teach Reading Well*. Portsmouth, NH: Heinemann.

Serravallo, Jennifer. 2015. *The Reading Strategies Book: Your Everything Guide to Developing Skilled Readers*. Portsmouth, NH: Heinemann.

Shannon, David. 2004. *A Bad Case of Stripes*. New York: Scholastic.

Shubitz, Stacey. 2016. *Craft Moves: Lesson Sets for Teaching Writing with Mentor Texts*. Portland, ME: Stenhouse.

Sullivan, Peter, and Pat Liburn. 2002. *Good Questions for Math Teaching: Why Ask Them and What to Ask*. Sausalito, CA: Math Solutions.

Tough, Paul. 2012. *How Children Succeed: Grit, Curiosity, and the Hidden Power of Character*. New York: Houghton Mifflin Harcourt.

Van de Walle, John, Lou Ann Lovin, Karen Karp, and Jennifer Bay-Williams. 2013a. *Teaching Student-Centered Mathematics: Developmentally Appropriate Instruction for Grades Pre-K–2, Volume I.* Pearson.

----------. 2013b. *Teaching Student-Centered Mathematics: Developmentally Appropriate Instruction for Grades 3–5, Volume II.* Pearson.

----------. 2013c. *Teaching Student-Centered Mathematics: Developmentally Appropriate Instruction for Grades 6–8, Volume III.* Pearson.

Wesson, Ken. 2001a. "A Conversation About Learning and the Brain-Compatible Classroom" hosted by Susan Kovalik and Associates, Federal Way, WA, January 12, 2001.

----------. 2001b. "What Recent Brain Research Tells Us About Learning." *Independent School*, 61(1):58.

Willis, Judy M.D. 2008. *Research-Based Strategies to Ignite Student Learning*. Alexandria, VA: ASCD.

CERTIFICATE OF COMPLETION

This is to certify that

____

has successfully completed 7 contact hours at the following workshop by The 2 Sisters:

CAFE: ASSESSMENT TO INSTRUCTION
Get Ready, Assess, and Teach Every Student
A Successful Way Forward to Literacy

______________________ ______________________

DATE LOCATION

Allison Behne
Assistant Professor of Education,
Upper Iowa University

STARTING OUT

CAFE OVERVIEW

CAFE MENU

ACCOUNTABILITY

CAFE SYSTEM

CAFE RESOURCES

RESOURCES

REFLECTION

My Intent...

HOPEFUL	SHINE	FORWARD
GRATEFUL	CONNECT	ENJOY
DARE	ABUNDANT	FLY
GRACE	BALANCE	ENCOURAGE
BRAVE	TOGETHER	INTENTIONAL
GROW	PRESENT	RESILIENCE
DISCOVER	EMPOWER	FOCUS
INVENT	DO	ALIGN
BOLD	DISCOVER	OPEN
DREAM	LEAP	ENOUGH
ELEVATE	INSPIRE	RESET
COMMIT	LEARN	ORGANIZE
CREATE	FINISH	THRIVE
CONFIDENCE	RESOLVE	REFRESH
FEARLESS	REACH	COMMITMENT
ACCEPT	CHOOSE	POSSIBILITY
FLEXIBILITY	HELP	TRUST
UPWARD	LIMITLESS	ONWARD

Reflection . . .

Takeaways from the Day...

Discover The Daily CAFE

These titles are all on TheDailyCAFE.com website. Put the title in the search engine to expand your learning.

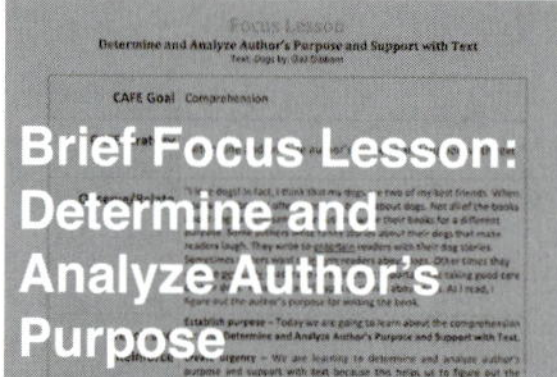

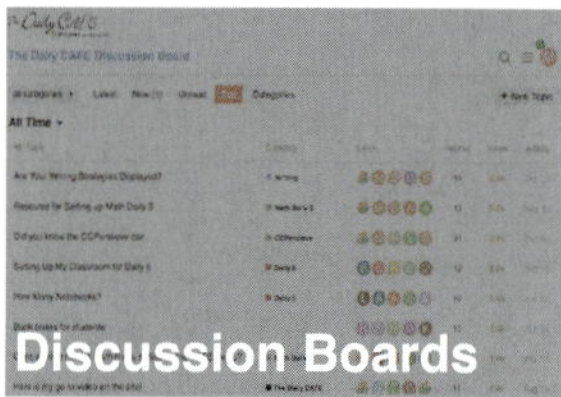

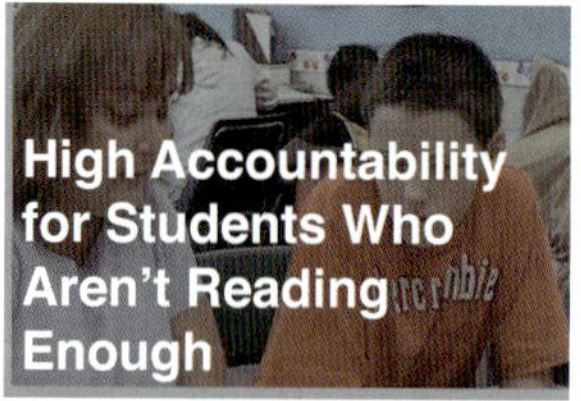

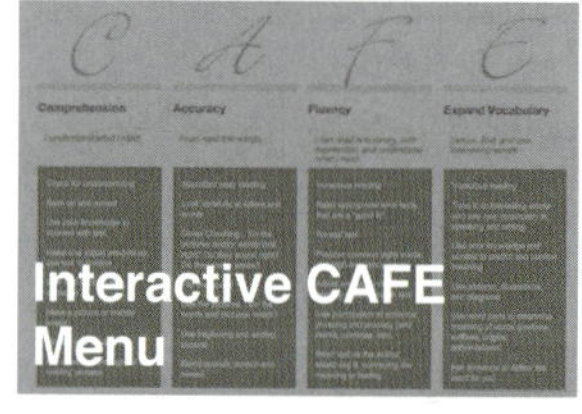

In one word or phrase, what will you search on TheDailyCAFE.com?

CAFE Book Study	Brief Focus Lesson